Contents

ALTERNATIVE DISPUTE RESOLUTION: THE FUTURE BEHOLDS (INDIAN PERSPECTIVE)

VOLUME 2, ISSUE 1 OF BRILLOPEDIA

TUSHAR KANTI MOHINDROO

ISBN 979-888606502-2

Preface

"Start writing, no matter what. The water does not flow until the faucet is turned on".

-Louis L'Amour

Hundreds of students and professors are contributing their work to Brillopedia, we are here to provide ample information about Law and Contemporary issues. Our aim is to provide a platform for today's generation to express their views and ideas on law and contemporary law.

Publication

This research paper is published in volume 2, issue 1 of Brillopedia

Author

Tushar Kanti Mohindroo

CHAPTER ONE

ABSTRACT

Alternative Dispute Resolution is a concept which comes under the blanket of the legal field, but with its own terms and conditions. This concept consist of various types of methods to resolve the legal staples minus involving the court or the traditional method of filing a case before a court of law. In India, the existence of ADR can be seen from past timeline in different names and forms, but a fully mapped legislation was made to support the technique of ADR, as the world was evolving to adopt this method more effectively and to work efficiently by several of conventions or conferences during the timeline in the 20th century. These means are not flawless and tend to be replaced from the traditional method as they also comes with their own issues and flaws.

As Mahatma Gandhi said "I realized that the real fiction of a lawyer is to unite the parties... Most of the time in 20 years of my practice in law has been spent making private compromises for hundreds of jobs, business. I didn't lose anything because of it, not even money, certainly not my soul"[1]. This statement simply puts the roots for the ADR in Indian perspective and in the motion for Alternative Dispute Resolution.

This paper accommodates deep to the roots of ADR in India, then with the study of ADR along with the types of ADR legalized in India with simultaneously explaining their issues/obstacles (PART I) ,along with the analysis of the current Indian Legal system and its issues or problems. Then there is a comparison between both the methods and a question is answered that out of both the methods which leads the future or which will be effective in future to provide citizens the justice they deserve (PART II). In the end, the PART III consists the conclusion of the whole paper along with the references used to complete the research.

[1] Mark Juergensmeyer, 'Gandhi Ways: A Handbook of Conflict Resolution.

CHAPTER TWO

INTRODUCTION

From the times even before any law was established, people who got in conflict used to bring in a third person for the motive to solve their issue and gave a valid and reasonable decision for the benefit of parties involved. It was a routine for the people as there was not any law, authority, court by bringing justice because of the absence of any authority over the people except the rules/decisions made by the king of that particular area. Those rules/decisions made by king were final and obeyed by his people and most of the time to solve a dispute or a conflict, a person was appointed may it be the king with any of his minister. This was the solitary system to solve the disputes or conflict of the people during the old times.

This system or now mechanism in the current timeline is called “Alternative Dispute

Resolution”. Various historians, philosophers, jurists and advocates have acknowledged this system around the globe even after the manifestation of a finely maintained and complicated judiciary system of their country or even on international level.

Alternative Dispute Resolution does not need any complicated explanation, it’s explanation is in its name itself as Alternative means ‘different but same aim or second’, a dispute is ‘any conflict/issue’ and resolution is ‘a firm/final decision’, thus by putting in simpler terms the definition can be ‘a mechanism which provides a firm decision to a conflict or an issue’. It keeps aside the traditional methods which are used to solve the matters which is the method of going to courts, filing a case, hearings, evidence and the wait for decision by the judge. The notion of ADR has the potential to replace traditional dispute resolution methods. ADR proposes to resolve all types of cases including civil, commercial, industrial, family etc. where people cannot enter into any negotiations and reach a settlement. Typically, ADR employs a neutral third party to help the parties communicate, discuss disputes and resolve disputes. It is a technique that allows individuals and groups to maintain cooperation, social order and the ability to reduce hostility.

Alternative Dispute Resolution is a way to solve the quarrels in an approach in which both the parties that are involved in most of the cases concludes with the no lose side.

This instrument offers righteousness in a simpler and tries to give effective result in a way, the real system which is mostly used to solve the disputes on a regular basis that aims to provide justice but with a complex process and take a lot of time to provide justice and fair decision.

However, this doesn't convey that, the ADR mechanism is better and have no flaws in it. This will be discussed and concluded that what the future says and how will both the mechanisms will get approached and chose by the people in seek of justice.

In India, the process of ADR is present in different forms from ancient times where the ministers along with their king (upon choosing) played the role of third person to give a final decision on the basis of significant parties, sometimes choose to resolve any family matter(s) by involving any old member of the family or old member of that area, sometimes in business related matters also.

In ADR, the word alternative contains all the several forms of mechanisms or we can say there are various types under ADR with their own methodology, advantages, flaws, etc. The major and recognized forms of ADR are: Arbitration, Mediation, Conciliation, Negotiation and LokAdalat (only in India) there are more forms of ADR but these are the major ones with different names all around the globe, these types are also legitimized in India and are fully authorized to work sovereignty. Further, in this paper all of the types which are recognized in India will be discussed along with their attributes.

In basic terms, ADR can be deliberated as a legit mechanism under the nose of the law established which solves the disputes may better than the authentic judiciary mechanism, which might get supplementary appreciation and approached by the people to grow the impartiality and righteousness they need within the reasonable means, time and money. As time saving, less expensive, less hassle, more effective, less biased are the major characteristics of the ADR mechanism.

CHAPTER THREE

ROOTS OF ADR IN INDIA

ADR has been in India through centuries, its roots can be traced back from various empires and dynasties. All are mentioned in brief below:

- **In Ancient India**

It is for the most part guessed that the overall arrangement of government that won in antiquated

India was the government, and this view depends on the undeniable discernment that since old India was the lord of rulers, the government framework existed. In any case, this was not the framework that was pervasive in antiquated occasions. In old occasions, questions were settled calmly through mediations of kulas (family or faction congregations), srenis (men's societies who followed a similar occupation and had a place with various groups and clans) gatherings or gatherings of traders and craftsmen who had a place with various clans, however the debates are by one way or another connected by their occupation.

Back in ancient periods, there were scores of mediation as 'Puga, Sreni and Kula'. There was a chain of importance of grumblings, the decision of the Kula or tribe bunch was submitted to survey by Sreni, which thus could be explored by Puga. From Puga an allure was made to Pradvivaca and ultimately to the ruler and the sovereign. Sreni additionally used to mediate in joint family debates between its individuals, which in were settled by their older folks if not settled. In case they were unfit to go to an understanding, the sreni or organization courts will additionally step in. Srenis, or societies, turned into an unmistakable element of crude India's business life around 500 B.C. They were efficient, to their own leader advisory groups of four or five people. This is hard to know the idea of the Gana Court. It's most presumably as old as' PugaCourt, which was overwhelmed by individuals from shifted social layers and callings who lived in a similar spot. It was obviously the well-known panchayat courts.[1]

- **During Mauryan Dynasty**

In 322 BC, Chandragupta Maurya became ruler of the Magdha region in North India, so with the assistance of his consultant Kautilya, he assembled a realm. The ruler was the head of equity during the line, and all matters were chosen by the ruler, yet at the nearby level, there were courts coordinated by individuals. In the little towns, unique courts managed by Mahatmas and Rajukas. No less than one court and one police base camp were made in all huge urban communities and central command. In supplement to these courts, trivial offenses in the towns were taken care of by town older folks in neighborhood panchayats. The Hindu code of law, as contemplated in the shastras, were implemented in civil matters.[2]

- **During Mughals**

The Mughals had three separate judicial authorities that worked simultaneously times and independently of each other and these are:

- religious law courts was headed by Quazis
- secular law courts under the direction of governors, faujdars, Kotwal and in Hindu cases passed to be ruled by Brahmins
- The political courts were ruled by subahdars, faujdars, kotwal, etc.;

Most of the villagers, however, settled their cases in the village courts themselves and appealed to the caste or panchayats courts, arbitration by an impartial arbitrator (salis). The emperor was the last court of appeal.

- **During the British rule**

Supervision in India was predominant below the British regime, the current legal system was very similar to that of British India. India's alternative dispute resolution picked up pace in with the arrival of the East Indian Society in 1857, classified the process of civil courts, except those proven by the Royal Charter, which enclosed Sections 326 & 327, They provided for arbitration without court intervention provided. After the making of provisions, Administrative Law of India, was enacted in 1899 which was made on the basis of the English Arbitration Act in 1889 this was the first shot to offer the substantive law on arbitration, but its submission was imperfect. However, the presidential city of Calcutta, Bombay and Madras had many shortcomings and attracted much criticism. After all this in 1940, the Arbitration Act was enacted, which amended the Indigenous Arbitration Act of 1899 and Section 89 and Sections (a) to (f) of Section 104 (1) and Second 1908 Civil Procedure Code List consolidated the Arbitration Act in British India and remained a comprehensive Arbitration Act in Republican India until 1996.

[1] Political Institutions & Administration, PB Udgaokar, Banarsidas Publications Pvt. Ltd., 1986, pg 209.

[2] http://www.preservearticles.com/2011101815640/essay-on-the-judicial-system-of-the-mauryan-rulers- india.html.

CHAPTER FOUR

LEGISLATION OF ADR

ADR is a well-practiced mechanism from centuries as discussed above, thus to acknowledge it in the current timeline, the legitimization of the mechanism should be discussed as what is the existing scenario of ADR in the eyes of law. To legitimize the mechanism, there are some legislative status given by the Indian law, by enacting special acts which are as follows:

- **Code of Civil Procedure**

The Code of Civil Procedure, 1859 in its segments 312 to 325 managed discretion in suits while areas 326 and 327 given to assertion without court intercession. The Code of Civil Procedure (Act 5 of 1908) canceled the Act of 1882. The CPC, 1908 has set out that cases should be urged to go in for ADR under segment 89(1). Under the First Schedule, Order XXXII A, Rule 3 an obligation is provided reason to feel ambiguous about the courts that it will make an undertaking to help the gatherings on the main occurrence, in showing up at a settlement in regard of the topic of the suit. The subsequent timetable contained preliminary mediation and introduced a short intervention without the inclusion of the court. Request I, Rule 1 of the Appendix builds up that if in a case every one of the gatherings concur that a question in the midst of them ought to be submitted to intervention, they might do so at any time before the pronouncement of the judgment; reach to the court for a referral order. This program was somewhat complementary to the provisions of Arbitration Act, 1899.

- **Arbitration Act, 1899**

This Act was highly influenced by that of the British Arbitration Act of 1889. It widened the definition of arbitration by defining "submission" simply "a written agreement to submit present and future disputes to arbitration, whether or not an arbitrator is identified therein".[1]

- **Arbitration (Protocol and Convention) Act of 1937**

This Act was enacted from the two conventions which were on Arbitration held at Geneva, which are:

- Geneva Protocol on Arbitration Clauses, 1923
- Geneva Convention on the Execution of Arbitral Awards, 1927

The foremost resolution to enact this act stood to contribute presence and acknowledgment with the protocol and convention of the Arbitration.

- **The Arbitration Act, 1940**

The main purpose of the Act of 1940 is to provide authority to the courts in case of Arbitration, this Act only dealt with the domestic arbitration. This Act states the involvement of courts in the course of arbitrary tribunals at three stages;

1. Prior to the mention of the dispute/matter,
2. During the length of the chronicles of the dispute/matter,
3. After the award was passed.

The Act also provided for (a) arbitration proceedings without court intervention, (b) arbitration with legal recourse in pending lawsuits, and (c) intervention in arbitration where no matter was pending in court.

Before an arbitral tribunal would rule on a dispute, intrusion of the arbitral tribunal was necessary to start the arbitration procedure. The actuality of a pact and a dispute had to be attested. Throughout the proceedings, the interference of the court was necessary to extend the time limit for granting the judgment.

Ultimately, before the award could be imposed, it had to be made the court's rule.[2] The basic functions of ADR also weren't met by this Act. The Act's ambit of Judicial Intervention compromised its fundamental purpose.[6]It lacked a quick, effective, and transparent system for resolving disputes resulting from overseas trade and investment transactions.[3]

- **Arbitration and Conciliation Act of 1996**

This Act was instituted to recreate and refine the recently sanctioned Act of 1940, and to supplant it with this new Act. The UNCITRAL Secretariat, the Asia-Africa Legal Advisory Committee (AALCC), the International Council for Commercial Arbitration (ICCA), and the International Chamber of Commerce (ICC) held an audit meeting in 1978, at which the members collectively concurred that it would be in light of a legitimate concern for global business discretion for UNCITRAL to make strides prompting the development of uniform guidelines for arbitral measures. The issue of consistency was to be settled, coming full circle with the reception of the model law by UNCITRAL on July 21, 1985. This is a wonderful heritage set by the United Nations to International Commercial Arbitration, which has impacted Indian Law. In India, Model Law has been taken on practically completely in the 1996 Act.

This Act obliterated and revoked every one of the three demonstrations (1899, 1937 and 1940). Its fundamental goal was to support and move the instrument of ADR which is practical and a fast change system for resolving the business or practically any questions/matters. It covers both homegrown intervention and global business discretion.

The progressions presented through the 1996 Act stood so radical that all the statute of the keep going 56 years on mediation stayed repetitive. The Government of India passed the 1996 Act by its own announcement and afterward broadened it by elective pronouncement prior to being at long last passed by Parliament without alluding to a parliamentary board of trustees.

VeerappaMoily additionally noted at the ADR Congress in 2010 that the 1996 Act, however being founded on worldwide standards, has so far shown to be lacking in tending to the necessities of the business local area in India for the convenient and fair goal of questions.

The Law Commission of India delivered a report on the 1996 Act's insight and recommended various corrections. The Government of India introduced the Arbitration and Conciliation (Amendment) Bill, 2003, in Parliament dependent on the Commission's suggestions. The law commission's standing council noticed that Bill's arrangements accommodated over the top intercession by the courts in arbitral techniques.

[1] ,Law and Practice of Arbitration and Conciliation (2nd ed., 2006), OP Malhotra, InduMalhotra,

[2] Krishna Sarma, MomotaOinam&AngshumanKaushik, "Development and Practice of Arbitration in India –Has it Evolved as an Effective Legal Institution", http://iisdb.stanford.edu/pubs/22693/No_103_Sarma_India_Arbitration_India_509.pdf, (March 5, 2012, 10:30 PM).[6]Hon'bleThiru Justice S.B. Sinha, Judge Supreme Court of India, 'ADR and Access to Justice: Issues and Perspectives.

[3] Justice R.S Bachawat's, LexisNexis, "Law of Arbitration and Conciliation", preface commentary, (3rd ed., 1999).

CHAPTER FIVE

TYPES OF ALTERNATIVE DISPUTE RESOLUTION – LEGITIMIZED IN INDIA

ADR in India, can be generally categorized into two sorts; Court based Annexures (Arbitration,

Mediation and Conciliation) and socially/community based dispute resolution mechanism (LokAdalat). Each type have its specific features and rules, advantages and disadvantages. Some of them are acknowledged by the court, not all require the presence of a lawyer. Some ADR methods are binding, which means that the parties cannot ignore the decision on the basis of whether they agree with the decision or not.

There are five types of mode of arbitration which are followed and practiced in India, which are as follows:

1. Arbitration
2. Mediation
3. Conciliation
4. Negotiation
5. LokAdalat

- **ARBITRATION**

Assertion is the thought of questions between the gatherings by a nonpartisan substance who hosts been settled by the gatherings as a judge and chooses the case. In India, the law overseeing this method of ADR is the Arbitration and Conciliation Act, 1996, in light of the UNCITRAL model from 1985.

The said Act doesn't depict Arbitration especially however overall, as it simply expresses that mediation implies some intervention whether oversaw by a long-lasting arbitral organization. It is a strategy wherein the question is submitted to an arbitral court which settles on a choice (an "grant") on the debate that is restricting on the gatherings. It is a private, for the most part casual and non-legal preliminary system for arbitrating questions. There are four necessities of the thought of intervention: an assertion arrangement; a squabble; a situation to an outsider for its assurance; and an honor by the outsider. The assertion cycle can't continue without a legitimate discretion understanding before the question emerges. In this settlement strategy, the gatherings allude their debate to at least one people called referees. The judge's choice is restricting on the gatherings and their choice is alluded to as the "Grant". The motivation behind assertion is to get an only settlement of debates out of court denied of the fundamental deferrals and expenses.

Arbitration also consists of different modes which are as follows:

i. Ad-hoc Arbitration

This is the mode of Arbitration wherever the court fixes, not involve or intervene in the

Arbitration, thus all the powers to conduct the proceedings, appointing arbitrators and other rules are with the parties involved. Thus, no involvement of courts will lead to more cost-effective, flexible and quicker approach to conduct arbitration and the awards also. The advantage is that, it is settled and arranged by the parties themselves.

v. Institutional Arbitration

An institutional discretion remains an assertion where, particular long-lasting foundation meddles and embraces the elements of help and association of the intervention in agreement with the headings of that organization. Only the name of the institution is there, the arbitrators within the institute attend the proceedings of the arbitration. Hence, the name is Institutional

Arbitration. Incorporation of book of rules in the "arbitration agreement" is one of the principle advantages of institutional arbitration. Institutional Arbitration, throughout the world, is recognized as the primary mode of resolution of international commercial disputes. It is an arbitration administered by an arbitral institution.[1]

v. Statutory Arbitration

At the point when a law expresses that if a question shows up in a specific case, it ought to be settled through mediation, the arbitral methods are known as "legal assertion." Section 2(4) of the Arbitration and Conciliation Statute 1996 states that, except for areas 40(1), 41, and 43, the arrangements of Part I will apply to any discretion directed under some other demonstration as a result in India.

v. Fast Track Arbitration

Quick track intervention is a period bound mediation with stricter regulatory standards which doesn't allow any time expansions and the going with delays, and the more limited time span length makes it more expense effective. In India, the Indian Council of Arbitration (ICA) thought of the idea of facilitated/quick track discretion, and its enactment enables the gatherings to demand that its arbitral court settle the matter inside the time period given. The Act of 1996 gives individuals the option to pick the most sped up proper system for their assertion, resulting in a speedy disposition of the arbitral order.[2]

- **MEDIATION**

Mediation is a method in which there is a mediator, an external person, neutral to the dispute, works through the parties to find a solution which is adequate to all of them.[3] The basic motive of mediation is to offer the parties with a chance to talk, converse and explore options aided by a neutral third party, to exhaustively determine if a settlement is possible.[4] Mediation is an alternative method of dispute resolution where a neutral third party pursues to help two or more parties reach an agreement. It is a simple and straightforward party-oriented negotiation process where a third party acts as a mediator to decide disputes amicably using proper communication and negotiation abilities. This process is fully controlled by the parties. It is the mediator's job to aid the parties to find a solution of their dispute. The mediator does not enforce his opinion or make a decision about what an equitable settlement should be.

The process of Mediation is into different stages, which are as follows:

- Opening Statement – by the appointed mediator
- Joint Session – inviting both the parties with their point of views and demands
- Separate Session – for understanding the dispute deeper
- Closing Statement – summarizing the facts, issues, decision is made by the mediator, and if he's unable to conclude the mediation then the decision is made with the help of techniques like; Best Alternative to Negotiated Agreement (BATNA), Most Likely Alternative to Negotiated Agreement (MLATNA) and Worst Alternative to Negotiated Agreement (WATNA)

In India, mediation is not yet very popular. One reason is that mediation is not a formal process and cannot be carried out by courts. Lack of initiative on the part of the government or other institutions to take action to promote and spread cognizance among the people in general. Thus, it is second mode on the choice between selecting the modes of ADR between issues by the parties.

- **CONCILIATION**

Conciliation is "a process in which a neutral person meets with the parties to the dispute which might be resolved; a relatively unstructured method of dispute resolve in which a third party facilitates communication between parties in an attempt to help them settle their differences".[5] This entails an attempt by a third party, designated by the appellants, to reconcile them either before they resort to litigation (whether to court or arbitration), or after. The attempt to conciliate is generally based on showing each side the contrary aspects of the dispute, in order to bring each side together and to reach a solution.[6]

This form of ADR is identical to arbitration but has a less structured process. It is the process of facilitating an amicable settlement among parties in conflict through the use of a conciliator who meets with the parties separately to end the actual problem. The conciliator meets privately with the parties to lessen tensions, increase communication, and interpret issues in order to reach a negotiated accord. There is no requirement for a prior agreement, and it cannot be enforced on parties who do not intend to compromise. This is the gap among conciliate and arbitration.

Accordingly, there is a thin line of difference between mediation and conciliation. While in meditation, the third party, neutral intermediary, termed as mediator plays more active role by giving independent compromise formulas after hearing both the parties; in conciliation, the third neutral intermediary's role, is to bring the parties together in a frame of mind to forget their animosities and be prepared for an acceptable compromise on terms midway between the stands taken before the commencement of conciliation proceedings.[14]

- **NEGOTIATION**

Negotiation for the purpose of persuasion-is the pre-eminent mode of dispute resolution. Compared to processes using mutual third parties, it has the benefit of letting the parties themselves to control the course and the resolution.[7]

Essentials of Negotiation are:

- It is a communication process;
- It resolves conflicts;
- It is a voluntary exercise;
- It is a non-binding process;
- Parties hold authority over result and procedure;
- There is a chance to achieve broad-reaching solutions and enhancing mutual gains.[8]

Sometimes, negotiation is measured to be a piece of mediation but it is wholly true. However, it is more universally denoted as a method by which the disputing parties will resolve their dispute on their own. The negotiation process offers the parties the opportunity to exchange ideas, identify troubling points of difference, find solutions and gain mutual commitment to reach a final agreement or decision. Negotiation is such a process which has no defined or particular set of rules, it has full freedom but on an anticipated pattern.

- **LOK ADALATS**

Lok Adalats are the community aided form of dispute resolution with zero involvement from the judges or establishments, this mode of ADR can be alleged as the oldest form present in India.

Article 39A of the Constitution provides "equal justice and free legal aid"[9]. From this, the enactment with the Legal Services Authorities Act was done in 1987 with the only motive to spread awareness about the act and providing assistance to the needy people who were unaware of their rights.

Honorable Delhi High court has set a landmark decision highlighting the significance of Lok

Adalat movement in the case of Abdul Hasan& National Legal Services Authority v. Delhi

Vidyut Board and Others.[10] The decision of the Hon'ble Court was to establish LokAdalats with permanent status.

On March 14th 1982, the 1stLokAdalat was organized at a domicile called Junagarh, Gujarat. It was the first, afterward this form of ADR gained more and more presence and with faster disposal of disputes people chose this mode over other options because of which, LokAdalat gained legal status through the Legal Services Authorities Act, 1986. Not only the legitimization of LokAdalat was there but provisions for providing free legal support was also focused but only to the people who could not afford the expenses of the traditional mechanism of court system. Further the Act, was amended in 2002, which helped in establishing various kinds of LokAdalats with the criteria of three intensities; Regular LokAdalats; Permanent LokAdalats and Permanent LokAdalats for six specific public utility services.

Whenever a dispute or a matter is given or goes into the channel of LokAdalats, generally two ways are to available, which are as follows:

1. If after hearing in the LokAdalat, the decision is of compromise/ cooperation, then the award will be given to the terms agreed by the parties involved,
2. If later inquiry in the LokAdalat, the decision to compromise is not attained then the parties are recommended to method the court laterally with the failed report of the LokAdalat.

There can be no other hybrid directive granted by the LokAdalat which contains directions to the parties. When there is no settlement, there can be no award. When there is no settlement, the LokAdalat cannot issue instructions defining the rights, obligations, or title of parties. The settlement should happen well before award, not the other way around.[11]

[1] A Consultation Paper, Proposed Amendments to Arbitration and Conciliation Act, 1996 Ministry of Law and Justice, Government of India, at p. 18.

[2] Section 11(2) and 13(2) of the Arbitration and Conciliation Act, 1996

[3]SriramPanchu, LexisNexis, Mediation: Practice and Law, p. 9, 2011.

[4]Madhubhushi Sridhar, LexisNexis Butterworths, Alternative Dispute Resolution: Negotiation and Mediation, p.

234, (1st edition, 2006)

[5] Garner, Black's Law Dictionary (9th ed., 2009)

[6] Mauro Rubino-Sammartano, Wolter's Kluwer (Pvt. Ltd.), New Delhi, International Arbitration Law and Practice, p. 7, (2nd ed., 2007) [14] Supra Note 7.

[7] Supra Note 18, p. 3 and 17.

[8] Supra Note 23, p. 163.

[9] Article 39A, the Constitution of India, 1949.

[10] AIR 1999 DEL 88.

[11] B.P. MoideenSevamandir vs. A.M. Kutty Hassan, AIR 2008 SC (Supp) 1123; State of Punjab vs. Jalour Singh, 2008 2 SCC 660.

CHAPTER SIX

CHALLENGES FOR ADR

Even after the formation of the Arbitration and Conciliation Act, 1996, there are some areas where the mechanism of ADR have remained left behind, some of the reasons or the challenges faced by the mechanism in India, are mentioned below:

- Orthodox mindset of Indians

Since India, is in the developing stages to being a fully developed country, thus the mindset of the people in India is somewhat towards the traditional way of going to courts for any dispute, this sums up the faith of the Indians which is negative in response to approaching the mechanism of ADR.

- Assertiveness

Since the mindset is not bended towards the mechanism, thus the main feature of ADR is to create a win-win situation, but Indians have the thinking that the ADR will be of the same procedure as the traditional i.e. the probability of losing and wining situation. Hence, the chi of ADR is under the complex radar of a strange process under the eyes of Indians.

- Lack of interest in clients

The conventional outlook drives clients in the legal field to prefer the old-fashioned means of contacting the courts, which creates less interest among potential clients in choosing the mechanism of ADR. This is in addition to the misinformation spread by lawyers/advocates, who influence even potential clients to choose the traditional procedure over the ADR process.

- Lack of proper laws/rules/guidelines

The act 'Arbitration and Conciliation Act, 1996' was last amended in 2015, this shows the irregularity in codifying and modifying the rules or guidelines for ADR. This is a setback for such a relief mechanism by nit giving proper time and changes during the evolving times. The law making authorities does not give much attention to this mechanism, this leads to the less enthusiasm and faith of people as a thought is there that if government and law makers are not inclined towards it then why they have to choose ADR.

- Lack of legal education

Individuals in India mainly does not know their basic rights which are available to them, then there is more probability that people would know less about the ADR mechanism which does have the attributes of being; cheaper, faster and time saving method to solve any issue. This challenge is also because of less skill based mediator, negotiator or arbitrator which are not trained well to make a situation of benefit for both the parties. Thus, it requires that any mode of ADR must be performed by a fully skilled and knowledge person who understands the ADR mechanism well, so that the dispute could be resolve in less time with winning of both the parties, so that the subsequent period they come back by choosing any mode of ADR.

- Intrusion of Courts in ADR proceedings

In India, the courts hold the supremacy to the rule of law and people tend to approach the courts, thus people and law makers in their sub-conscious leans towards the interference of court even in the proceedings of ADR, it provides the people a sign of faith towards the court and security of their case/dispute as the involvement of the court will mark the people count faith on the decision of their ADR proceedings. This leads to restrict the basic feature of ADR of working freely and with no restrictions, mere involvement is okay with the process as mentioned in Section 34 under the Arbitration and Conciliation Act, 1996[20] stating the application to the court in the matter involving setting aside and modifying the decision/arbitral award. This is a complex challenge in growth of ADR, as there are number of cases challenging the legality of the section concerned, as in a landmark case of

McDermott International Inc. v. Burn Standard Co. Ltd.[21] it was stated by the Supreme Court that the Arbitration Act only provides a monitoring over the functions of Arbitration not the whole control and interference of the Court and by modifying or setting aside any decision by the arbitrator demands the ability of the arbitrator which is voidable in nature, this case is used further in various cases involving the issue of the said section.

CHAPTER SEVEN

INDIAN JUDICIAL SYSTEM

The Indian Judiciary System, is the furthermost 'simple yet complex' mechanism that aims to provide justice to the people of India, by adjudicating the matters or disputes according to the law of land. As India is a country of 29 states & 7 union territories, each state have its own law governed by the state administration and union territories under the governance of the central government. Thus, both state and union territory enjoys some judicial powers by establishment of several courts as provided by the Constitution of India. The judiciary system is hierarchal in nature consisting of majorly three levels of courts. The topmost in the hierarchy with the most powers is the Supreme Court or referred as 'Apex Court', situated in Delhi and second are the High Courts of the states & union territories and third on the hierarchy are the Districts Courts within the states consisting of various level of jurisdiction and distinction.

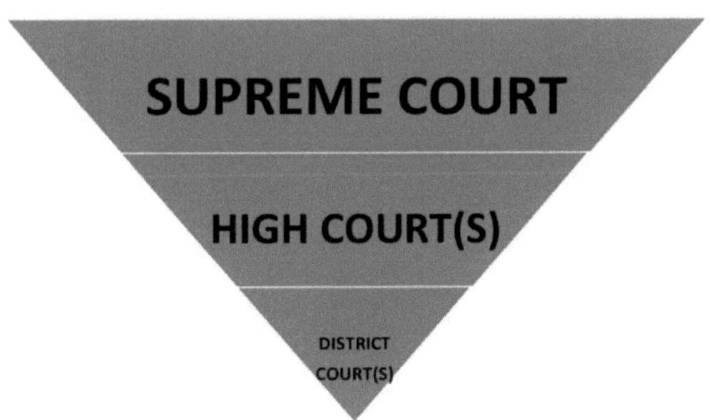

The above inverted pyramid chart is the depiction of the hierarchal system of courts in India in which the broadest section consist of the Supreme Court showing the authority that the court have, the second section is of High Court(s) showing less powers than the Supreme Court & the last section is of District Courts showing the least powers in this system.

- **Provisions regarding the Judiciary**

The main provisions regarding the upkeep of judiciary are specified in the Constitution of India, which delivers for:

- the establishment of the Supreme Court of India, its constitution, organisation, constitutional jurisdiction and powers, qualifications for the appointment of judges, method of appointment, their conditions of service and security of tenure[1],
- the establishment of a High Court for each state or more states, its constitution, organisation, constitutional jurisdiction and powers, qualifications for appointment of judges, method of appointment, their conditions of service and security of tenure[2],
- The vesting of effective administrative control in the High Court, over the subordinate judiciary, and in the matter of enrollment of personnel to the judicial services[3].

According to Article 245 and Article 245(1), "Subject to the provisions of this Constitution, Parliament may make laws for the whole or any part of the territory of India, and the Legislature of a State may make laws for the whole or any part of the State."[25]

- **Characteristics of Judiciary**

Indian Judiciary contains quite a few features, which describes this organ of the government very thoroughly, some of the important characteristics are as follows:

- Single & Integrated System - The constitution creates a unified integrated judicial system for all of India. The Supreme Court of India is the highest court in the country and below it are the state high courts. Other courts (subordinate courts) operate under higher courts. The Supreme Court controls and directs the track of justice in India. All Indian courts are associations of a single legal system.

- Independent body – The constitution supports the judiciary to be an independent body without dependency on any other body or institution. Providing, the appointment of judges only by the President, Removal of any judge through impeachment, the functional autonomy, etc., these such points make the judiciary an independent body.
- Interpreter of the Constitution – The Apex Court or Supreme Court enjoys the right to interpret and to clarify[4] which is backed by the Constitution, it is the final interpreter of the law which are provided in the provisions of the Constitution.
- Judicial Review – Supreme Court is considered the guardian of the Fundamental Rights and the liberty of the people. To perform this duty, it exercises the power of judicial evaluation. Supreme Court partake the power to reject any law and clamp unconstitutional with reasonable objection, High Courts also enjoys the same power.
- Judicial Activism - The Indian judicial system is becoming increasingly active. The Supreme Court has issued judicial decisions and directives designed to actively protect the public notice & human rights. The judiciary has instructed public officials to better protect public rights. The PIL system has gained momentum.
- Public Interest Litigation System - Under this system, Indian courts can take and enforce actions to safeguard a significant public or general interest that is or might be exaggerated by the action of any public or set apart power. Accordingly, any citizen or group or a non-profit association or even a court can bring to the front any case that requires measures to protect and satisfy the interest at large. It further provides a simple, simple, fast and economical scheme to provide legal assistance to the community that has been harmed.
- Establishment of High Court for each state as well as Joint High Court(s)[5]
- Supreme Court as the arbiter of disputes/issues between the union and states[28]

Above stated points are the features of the Indian Judiciary supported by the Constitution, and evolved through landmark judgments along with the timeline.

[1] Articles 32, 136, 132, 133, 139A, 141, 143, 124-127 of the Constitution of India.

[2] Article 214-231 of the Constitution of India.

[3] Article 233-237 of the Constitution of India. [25] The Constitution of India, 1949

[4] AIR (1973) 4 SCC 225.

[5] Article 214 of the Constitution of India, 1949.[28] Article 131 of the Constitution of India, 1949.

CHAPTER EIGHT

ISSUES WITH INDIAN JUDICIARY

Judiciary enjoys number of powers provided by the Constitution, and all the features of the judiciary involving the independent body and integrated system, there are some shortcomings of the organ to provide justice with the time evolved, there are causes for not as much of effect of judiciary, which are as follows:

- **Pendency of Cases at all the levels**

This has stood a major blow for the working of the judiciary, as the amount of pending cases are getting increased on a daily basis, as the judiciary have failed to provide justice on time. The foremost cause for pendency is because of the less working mechanism of judges along with the less strengths of judges. As of 2015, the pendency of cases in all the High Courts and that of district courts were around 2.07 crores with 17.6 lakh in High Courts [1] whereas the remaining 1.89 crores were in district and session courts.[2]

And as per current statistics of the Supreme Court compiled till 01/10/2021, were total of 69,922* cases were pending only in Supreme Court in which 51,581 cases were admission matters and 18,341 were hearing matters.[3]

According to data obtained as of 10/09/2021, there are a total of 10686745 civil cases outstanding and 29397587 criminal cases pending, taking the total number of cases pending in Indian courts to 40084332 or 4 crore plus cases.[4]

The Chief Justice of India, NV Ramana, has expressed his concern about the rise in case pendency, with the goal of making mediation a mainstream practise, which would aid in clearing the logjam of incomplete cases that are preventing the courts from working without pressure.[5]

- **Corruption**

As per the other pillars of democracy, the executive & the legislative, the judiciary has also (in some cases) encountered corruption. No accountability system has been established. In judicial proceedings, even the media are unable to convey an adequate and clear image of the corruption scene. The media seems to be more focused on exposing corruption in other areas, particularly in the executive branch. A minister who takes bribes or distributes money in elections may make headlines, but a court clerk who takes bribes and changes the trial date goes unnoticed.

According to the constitutional provision, there is still no provision to register an FIR against a judge who has accepted bribes without seeking the permission of the Chief Justice of India. Obviously, it is not what a poor person will prefer to attend the CJI, obtain his permission and then register an FIR. This will be extra costly and time consuming for him, in addition to court and legal fees. The professional arrogance of the judges, in which the judges do not do their duties and make serious decisions ignoring judicial precedents or principles, delays justice and increases the spam of the trials. In 2011, SoumitraSen, a former Calcutta Supreme Court judge, became the first judge in India to be charged with embezzlement by RajyaSabha.

To highpoint the concern which was in ancestries from decades, former Chief Justice

Venkataramiah who was the 19th Chief Justice, from June 19, 1989 to December 17, 1989, told a journalist KuldipNayar on his eve of retirement that “The judiciary in India has deteriorated in its standards because such judges are appointed as are willing to be ‘influenced by lavish parties and whisky bottles”. [6]

- **Lack in transparency in appointment of judges**

The collegiate system and the new system that the government is attempting to build for the selection of judges, the NJAC, have recently sparked debate across the country. Neither the university system nor the NJAC appear to be transparent enough to ensure that the process of selecting judges is clear and understandable to citizens. All democracies are moving rapidly towards open government and the right of citizens to information, an international trend that is increasingly supported by decisions of judiciary. Additionally, the right to information is considered a part of freedom of speech and mien, and the current secrecy system, as implemented by the university system, encroach upon the said fundamental right. The principles of open procedure and justice are fundamental for an equitable administration of justice.

The current government, headed by Prime Minister NarendraModi, says that the introduction of NJAC should bring more transparency to the appointment of judges. However, the Supreme Court of India deprived of the fact, saying that an even higher level of law required for judges to be appointed because the NJAC was not "perfect". According to the SC, the Advocates Council has been asked to amend the NJAC to require that the committee consist of the Chief Justice of India and four senior Supreme Court judges.

The Constitution only provides for the President to appoint the Supreme Court justices in consultation with the Supreme Court of India & supplementary Supreme Court justices as he deems necessary.[7] However, the Constitution does not speak of what opinion will prevail in case of divergence or even bestowing to the precise criteria for the assortment of judges. We are talking about violating the independence of the judiciary, but we have obligation to understand that its independence is not first from political and executive influences, but also after the independence of the judiciary in terms of its vices and dominion.

- **Problems of under trial Accused**

Added shortcoming that arises from the above issues is the trial against the defendant. Exactly, it's acceptable for those who have committed a crime, but is it fair for an innocent person to spend more time in prison just to await their trial? Indian jails are full of indicted people; they are locked up in jails until their case is finalized. Most of the time, they spend more time in prison than they would have actually been granted if the case had been at some point and under the assumption that it had been definite in contradiction of them. Plus, all the cost, pain, and agony they use to defend themselves in court is worse than serving the actual sentence. According to court procedures, they are not guilty until sentenced. On the last indicator, the rich and powerful can turn the police on their side, and the police can harass or silence the poor and uncomfortable during lengthy court trials.

This tricky betrays the right to liberty from the accused under trials as the pendency of cases and incompetency of judges would lead to the destruction of lives of those who are under trials for number of years or even decades without any final decree or judgement.

As apiece the statistics from the government, in the year 2019, the total number of prisoners were

4, 78,600, out of which 3, 30,487 prisoners[8] were under-trial, which shows that approximately 69.05% are under-trial prisoners who have not gotten their due and justice within time and are serving as prisoners from years or even decades.

- **Strength of Judges**

By the growth in pendency cases, the main reason for that, is the less strength of the judges with according to the court and per person. All three level of courts lack the quantity of judges required to attend the cases pending or new ones. Thus, the less quantity leads to less quality and ultimately leads to the pendency of cases & absence of justice. This does not says that the current number of judges are totally incapable of clearing the backlogs, but the current number of judges are already stacked up fully and overloaded with work which leads to floundering disposing of cases.

- **Covid-19 Crisis**

In March, 2020, the virus of Covid-19 got declared as an epidemic situation by WHO, which led to nation-wide lockdown that led to the country at a still, which also included the halt of working of the Courts too for months nonetheless the courts were then started through online mode, but that halt led to pile up of more cases in the courts and further to that, the online court mechanism was considered to be complex as it was not habitual for everyone who was involved in the judiciary.

[1] As per statistics compiled by Indiastat, accessible at, www.indiastat.com/crimeandlaw/6/courts/72/highcourts/17696/ stats.aspx.

[2] Supra Note 41.

[3] Statistics compiled by the Supreme Court, accessible at https://main.sci.gov.in/statistics.

[4] Data accessible at, https://njdg.ecourts.gov.in/njdgnew/?p=main/pend_dashboard.

[5] Comments accessible at, https://www.news18.com/news/explainers/explained-cji-ramana-says-4-5-crore-casespending-heres-what-has-been-fuelling-backlog-3977411.html.

[6] Interview details accessible at, https://thewire.in/law/attorney-general-kk-venugopal-arun-mishra-prashant-bhushan.

[7] Article 124(2) of the Constitution of India, 1949

[8] Compiled data accessible at, https://ncrb.gov.in/sites/default/files/Executive-Summary-2019.pdf.

CHAPTER NINE

COMPARISON OF BOTH THE MECHANISMS

From the above deliberated explanations of both the mechanisms of ADR and the judicial process. A study of these mechanisms is required to attain the objective of this paper. This assessment will be in form of a table, stated under:

JUDICIAL PROCESS/COURT SYSTEM	ADR (ARBITRATION & MEDIATION)
These are court proceedings in which a third party (judge / other authority) decides on the outcome.	ADR comes with various mechanisms with their own rules and norms, for example, Arbitration is a quasi-judicial process and mediation is a cooperation process with no adjudicating authority.
Governance and procedure under the provisions of the allied statutes.	Arbitration is ruled by a single Act (Arbitration and Conciliation Act, 1996), whereas mediation is not governed under any kind of law or statute.
Compulsory binding of the decision on the parties.	An award is given under the Arbitration, in mediation a binding settlement is there only if the parties are agreed upon.
Focus is on past events with determination of rights and liabilities of parties involved.	Collaborative in nature, focus on creating a win-win situation for the parties involved.
Proceedings are public and which follow strict stages of procedures.	Proceedings are private with restricted stages (arbitration) and informal proceedings (mediation).
The final decision is appealable.	An award can mostly be challenged (arbitration) or the order of settlement cannot be challenged (mediation).
Involvement of fee structure by the court.	Involvement in arbitration and refundable fess in case of mediation.
No confidentiality, as the case are open to public even the evidence.	Strictly confidential process, only private procedures, except LokAdalat.

From the above table, it can be seen that the judicial process is much more of a restricted and public at the same time, ADR mechanisms are flexible and free from any restrictions.

Court measures are an important tool in the judiciary. It also describes the limits within which judges must exercise due caution to avoid such criticism and provide the intended redress mechanism without exceeding the limits recommended by the preserved constitution.

Each of the ADR processes has its own logic, purposes and jurisdiction. It should be less technical and more in the canons of justice and fair play, and get the referee to adhere to procedures and rules that build trust, not only by doing justice between the parties, but by doing so, it contributes the feeling of that justice seems to be plentiful. They have been completed, and this is being done vigorously. As the Conciliation, Negotiation and LokAdalats are the other forms under ADR, each have its own uniqueness and way to solve disputes. As in Conciliation, an assessor is there to give the final order, in Negotiation, a facilitator is appointed to give the final order and in LokAdalats are the community authorized members that would provide the latest decision for the dispute which is governed by the Legal Services Authorities Act, 1986. Thus there are a number of options accessible to the parties to hand-pick from these different mechanisms while in the court system, there is no option or choice for the party and have to file the case whatever the jurisdiction of the case demands.

The stated assessment of both the mentioned mechanisms, ADR & the judicial process, it is indecisive to give a result and come to a decision, as equally the mechanisms have their advantages and disadvantages, their own set of laws, regulations, etc. The issues or the challenges for both the mechanisms are different from each other, thus it can be said to a point that both the mechanisms are two sides of a coin, along with their main objective to provide justice on time and in feasible manner.

Thus, it tips to a big question of which instrument can be better in future for providing justice to people in the most effective manner. This paper main's objective is to give a point of suggestion on this question, which is mentioned below.

CHAPTER TEN

WHO LEADS THE FUTURE?

This is an immense question in the legal fraternity that available of the two options, which mechanism will be helpful and effective in providing the desired justice on time with fair methods.

India is a vast country, where there are people of different religions, caste, etc. Subsequently there are various laws and regulations which are accordingly created by the states for the betterment of their people, hence the states try to bring out the best for their people to receive justice effectively, but the procedures, the laws are only on paper in the practical world things are quietly the opposite and against the strategies and goals of the state as well as the central government. The mechanism of judicial process running from ages have botched the aim of providing justice on time, as justice delayed is justice denied, we all have heard this statement, hence the court system is on a back foot right now and failing continuously to decrease and abolish the issues which are slowing down the judicial process.

On the other side, ADR is a mechanism which is not governed by any authority except the Arbitration, thus it gives some merits and demerits also, merits can be the flexibility, cheaper, fast way resolving, and some demerits can be the biasedness of the chosen third person, nonappealable, etc. Thus it, shows that the ADR mechanism is not a fully secured way to thrive for justice. Rather, it needs some modifications and more regulation which can grace the mechanism not to restrict it just like the traditional judicial process.

To acquire the finest out of each mechanism, there are some improvements that need to be filling out the issues and reduce the challenges for smooth running of the mechanisms.

Improvements for the judicial process:

i. Increase in number of Courts and Judges – The most natural way to bring change is through the root of problems which is the deficiency of number of current judges and limited number of courts in the country.
ii. Giving financial autonomy to the Judiciary – That the planning and budgetary decisions must be finalized with due involvement of the judges, as they know better what could be done for the objective.
iii. Procedural Improvements – The trials of the court, requires to be more feasible and in a simple manner, with less complexity, the discretion power given to judges needs to be more independent and less comprehensive.
iv. Fixing time barrier – A regulation must be there that would put a time barrier for solving a dispute or case, for instance – A criminal case must be disposed within a span of 3 years or any time which will be reasonable for a particular case, depending upon the decidendi of the judge.
v. Restrictions on Adjournments – Presently, there is a rising trend of giving adjournments by judges due to very nominal reasons, like an advocate is not present for a party, any party is not attending the proceedings, etc. This trend need to be stopped and full restrictions must be there, which will not delay in the decision of the court.

Improvements for ADR:

I. Making people aware - One of the objectives should be to promote arbitration and thus prevent private players from rushing to court without resorting to the relevant arbitration rules. If people do not know their rights, they will never be able to seek justice. With this in mind, it is very important for us to raise awareness about arbitration, its needs and its importance.
II. Introduction of proper rules/regulations – Only law related to Arbitration is there but of 1986, which desires to be amended on a penurious basis and should not be ignored, whereas of other forms does not have any regulations, which needs to persistently brought for getting the faith of the people in choosing the ADR mechanism.
III. Compulsory ADR – No specific institution is there that would co-operate with the ADR internationally or nationally, thus the establishment of such institution must be there and agreements must include such institution that would make the agreements more secure.

IV. Less interference of the Courts – Alternate Dispute Resolution, in its name it suggest the option to not going to the Court and solving dispute through different forms, thus there must be slightest participation of the courts possible, so that the operational and working of these forms of ADR can be done with most effectiveness and efficiently.

The times of Covid-19 have brought single major change in both the mechanisms, as in judicial process the medium of online proceedings was adopted that brought a significant adjustment in the functioning of the judiciary even filing could be through internet, same in the case of ADR, another mechanism was formed as 'ODR' which is Online Dispute Resolution, that would lead the dispute resolution concluded medium of online or internet. It was a chaotic situation for the entire domain and in the legal world also as the lack of appropriate funds to fully go online with the courts brought other problems and controversies, another challenge to the judicial process, whereas the ODR got chosen more as it was more simple and more advanced approach than e-courts. This shows that ADR can work more efficiently than the court process even in a situation of a pandemic.

From the overhead conferred points, a clear image is present before us, as the subjects of both the mechanism needs more solutions, both needs major changes, both are reliable process for receiving justice, but somewhere in future with more demand from people and the increase in count of cases, the burden of the courts will be extra hence the courts will themselves recommend to choose ADR for solving the disputes on time and effectively. Thus, the mechanism of Alternate Dispute Resolution will be preferred more than the traditional judicial process in the future, this do not mean that the judicial process shall be forgotten or ignored, this means that the resolutions mentioned above, essentially be brought to improve the mechanism of the courts, so that all the pressure must not be transferred to the different forms of ADR, otherwise, in near future, ADR will also be in burden of pending cases just like the courts of India right now.

Therefore, the answer to the question is that the, ADR can be leading the future of the legal measures in India beside with the support of the court structure of the country, but with a catch to take duly diligence in criminal matters, if proceeded with ADR (only in future).

CHAPTER ELEVEN

CONCLUSION

From the above discussed, it shows the major problem of rising of pending cases in the judiciary, the slow work mechanism of the judiciary. The judicial process needs to bring a lot of changes in their mechanism as mentioned above, thus without these changes the current pile of problems will increase enormously within no time. Major efforts are required to bring and implement these changes as soon as possible, this can only be done the straight up efforts from the government that would bring major reforms in the judicial process which further will lead to a decay in the current problems of judicial way that would ultimately impact as a positive for people's faith in the judiciary. Notwithstanding, with the issues of judicial process, the common man of India have a never-ending faith in the judiciary, which is the biggest asset for the judiciary that the people supports the courts.

Similarly, ADR is quite the opposite process, where there are only minimal problems to which solutions are also mentioned above, issues for ADR mechanisms are of permanent in nature as the improvements for these problems would not remove the problems from its core rather it will make them invisible in nature, for instance the issue of less awareness or less demand cannot be abundantly detached as the judicial process would still be the first opinion of the general public of India, due to their faith and orthodox thought of mind. Thus, creating awareness would impact somewhat around 80-90% from total population to choose ADR but those 10-20% would still be there who have confidence in the court system, which is not wicked at all.

The future of ADR, totally depends upon the requirement of some rules and regulation which are needed to be brought, so no exploitation could be there. Along with the proper knowledge of the directions and approaches to the arbitrator, mediator, etc. whatever the party choose the form of ADR proper supervision and information must be there for each side and the authoritative person.

As proper forms of ADR when used appropriately will lead to take-over the overload of the problems for the judiciary which will help the country to have belief on getting justice.

Printed by Libri Plureos GmbH in Hamburg,
Germany